Historic Homes
of
AMERICA

Photography
Ric Pattison

Design
Teddy Hartshorn

Captions
Laura Potts

Director of Production
Gerald Hughes

CLB 2638
© 1992 Colour Library Books Ltd., Godalming,
Surrey, England.
All rights reserved.
This edition published in 1992 by
SMITHMARK Publishers Inc.,
16 East 32nd Street, New York, NY 10016.
Printed and bound in Singapore.
ISBN 0 8317 4476 6

SMITHMARK books are available for bulk
purchase for sales promotion and premium use.
For details write or telephone the Manager of
Special Sales, SMITHMARK Publishers Inc.,
16 East 32nd Street, New York,
NY 10016; (212) 532-6600.

Historic Homes of AMERICA

Text by
ERNEST WOOD

Photography by
RIC PATTISON

SMITHMARK

CONTENTS

INTRODUCTION

Previous page: Mount Vernon, the family home of
George Washington. Facing page: the Governor's Palace,
in Colonial Williamsburg.

Twenty years ago, when American historic preservation was just catching on strong, *New York Times* architecture critic Ada Louise Huxtable wrote an old house epitaph that told an all-too-familiar story:

"See the 116-year-old historic house. See it being knocked down. See the hamburger stand take its place. Pow. America, of thee I sing; sweet land of Burger King."

Funny? Yes. Sad? Even more so. Because this was a true story. Mapleside, a big, classically-designed sandstone house in Madison, Wisconsin, was gone forever.

So are half of the 200 buildings that the *Historic American Buildings* survey, a Depression-era program to find and document historic structures, identified in Mobile, Alabama.

So are thousands more historic buildings across America.

But there is good news. Because the other half of Mobile's historic buildings remain, and many of them have been restored. Because just down the highway in New Orleans, 10 districts containing more than 30,000 old buildings – mostly houses – have been officially recognized as historic and worth saving. Because in tiny Georgetown, Colorado, an old silver mining town that's not as big now as it was in its heyday, restored homes are key to preserving the unique character of the place.

Because for the last 20 years, America has had a love affair with old houses.

There always has been a small number of history buffs, genealogists and architects who admired and respected America's historic architecture. "Little old ladies in tennis shoes" were famous for lobbying against demolition. There were always a number of people who steadfastly preserved their own family homes. Many were "too poor to paint, too proud to whitewash," as the saying goes, but their pride saved many a house. And there always were certain houses and other buildings that were so historically significant that everyone agreed they should be saved. These buildings taught history lessons to millions of vacationing Americans every year.

The difference today is in the number of people who value old homes.

We've all heard it many times: Home is The American Dream. Finding a newer and better place to live is what brought most European settlers here in the first place. And it's what kept the pioneers pushing west. Many dwellings were crude in the early years. But the settlers who found fortune on the frontier built very fine homes indeed. Just keeping the rain off and the cold out were not enough. Americans wanted comfort and beauty in their homes. They wanted their dream.

Today, Americans still dream of the ideal home. They are curious about how other people live. They're curious about how people lived in the past. And they're curious about what it would be like to live that way themselves. Historic houses provide the perfect window.

Ever since air conditioning focused living inside and eliminated many of the reasons why houses should be different across the country, the need has been growing for the insights that old houses provide. Old houses can tell us about more than architectural style. They can tell us about the local economy, climate, ethnic heritage and aspirations. Urban row houses are brownstone in New York, graystone in Chicago and wood in San Francisco. Plantation owners built big Georgian houses in Virginia, modest Greek Revival houses in North Carolina and showy townhouses in Mississippi.

Ever since new buildings began to obliterate the past, the realization has also been steadily growing that what we're talking about is much bigger than a few old houses. Historians and preservationists in New Orleans don't see their historic homes as thousands of individual structures. The city has an official policy of regarding them *tout ensemble*, all together. Taken this way, historic houses are the tangible elements that create cities and give them their character. They are, in fact, the most tangible record of our past.

Whether seen individually or as a unit, historic houses are a record of American taste and lifestyle. And the individual historic house remains the basic building block of preservation. Houses are The American Dream. And Americans love their houses. As Mark Twain wrote: "Our house … had a heart, and a soul, and eyes to see us with. …We never came home from an absence that its face did not light up and speak out its eloquent welcome …."

THE HISTORY OF HOUSES
The earliest settlers in America worried about basic shelter, and they put up their houses quickly. These early structures

were not designed to last. They were not designed for beauty. They were designed to keep the elements out. When settlers did have time to build permanently, they naturally used the construction techniques and the styles that they had brought from home. That was the beginning of local styles. The Dutch built differently from the English, who built differently from the French, who built differently from the Spanish. Add to that the difference in building materials from region to region, and you have the beginnings of American regional architecture.

These differences created local styles, whether the builders realized it or not. An adobe house built by a Spanish monk in Texas couldn't help but be different from a wood frame house built by a Puritan in Massachusetts. You'll often hear people refer to a "Colonial" style house, though Colonial properly describes only the historical period when the American colonies belonged to different European nations. There was no such thing as Colonial style. At least there wasn't one colonial style that was common to the West, the South, New England and other regions.

It wasn't long, however, before American settlers began consciously to design their houses after fashionable styles. Over the coming years, they built in three basic styles: Classical, based on the traditions of Greece and Rome; Renaissance Classical, based on Italian inspiration; and Medieval, based on the Gothic. There were dozens of variations, however, from Jeffersonian (Classical) to Italianate (Renaissance) to Queen Anne (Gothic). And that's not counting the independent traditions of the Spanish and the Native Americans. Or the occasional short-lived oddity such as Egyptian style or the Octagon.

As the Dutch pulled out of the New World and the French and Spanish established themselves principally in Louisiana, the West and Canada, English architectural styles dominated the East Coast colonies that were to become the core of the United States. At first, architecture changed slowly. The Renaissance-based Georgian style, imported from England, dominated the 1700s. After the Revolution, however, Americans seeking their own identity created a local variation on Georgian called the Federal Style. By the 1820s Federal gave way to the Greek Revival, which Americans embraced with open arms, believing that since the Greeks had invented democracy, their style of architecture was the most appropriate for the new American Democracy. The pace quickened. At about 10-year intervals, new styles appeared, from the early Gothic Revival in the 1830s to picturesque cottages in the early 1840s to Italian villas in the late 1840s. And on and on.

Styles were spread by pattern books, which presented drawings and plans of the most up-to-date look in houses. Asher Benjamin's *The Country Builder's Assistant*, published in 1797, illustrated Federal style houses. Thirty years later, his *The American Builder's Companion* promoted the Greek Revival style. Andrew Jackson Downing's *Cottage Residences*, published in 1842, promoted small but richly-ornamented, picturesque Gothic houses. O.S. Fowler's 1853 book *The Octagon House: A Home for All* promoted more than a style; it promoted the eight-sided house as an efficient and healthy way to live.

By the Civil War – and for the rest of the history of American housing – there were so many ideas about house design that there always was some overlap, when more than one style was popular at a time. As a result, the late 19th century saw everything from French Second Empire to Richardsonian Romanesque, from Stick Style to Queen Anne and from Shingle Style to Beaux Arts. And the early 20th century saw revivals from Georgian to Tudor to Spanish Colonial and new styles that included Mission, Pueblo, Prairie and Bungalow.

Meanwhile, each style took on its own variations according to where and when it was built and who built it. Some builders learned of new styles from seeing other builders' work rather than from pattern books. Some learned styles when they were new, while others learned of them years later. Immigrants continued to bring their own traditions with them. (The log cabin, often considered an American type of building, came from Sweden; Charleston's tiered porches, known locally as piazzas, came from Barbados and the Caribbean.) And local building materials and local climate forced them to create new traditions. Each builder added his own touches. The many building materials, from wood to stone to brick to sod, and the many parts of a house, from the foundation to the windows, the chimneys, the porches and the roof, produced an endless variation in American houses.

The result was not so much an American architectural melting pot as a rich flowering of many parallel traditions. In San Antonio, German and Mexican immigrants each built from the local stone, but the results are remarkably different. The colonnades of the Greek Revival that had begun as a homage to democracy soon found favor in the South because they provided shade for a house during the steamy summertime.

Later, industrialization and the railroad made it easier to manufacture and ship building materials. Some components, such as windows, became standardized. The power-driven jigsaw made decorative flights of fancy commonplace. But changes in the building process – especially the switch from heavy timber construction to the light, easily-built balloon frame – revolutionized construction still more. Now, builders could put up houses of nearly any shape. And they could get the parts to produce any style that caught their eye. Does the client want a Georgian house?

Or an Italian villa? No problem. The materials, technology and historical precedents were available for both nearly anywhere, from the mountains of North Carolina, where George Vanderbilt put up a French chateau he called Biltmore, to the coast of California, where William Randolph Hearst built his own pleasure palace, San Simeon. Does the client want to update or enlarge the house? This is no problem either. Many is the mansion with a humble beginning – even a log cabin – buried inside the walls.

Eclecticism continued well into the 20th century. In fact, it never really died. Despite the modern movement, houses have continued to be built in traditional styles: Georgian, Tudor, Greek Revival. There's something about historic homes that Americans have always loved. Something they continue to love.

PRESERVING HOUSE HISTORY

Americans began their love affair with old buildings early. By 1812, plans were being made to reconstruct the steeple on Independence Hall. The Philadelphia City Council justified the work (which was finally completed 17 years later) as a matter of patriotism. But the preservation projects Americans really loved were old houses. In 1853, a South Carolina woman named Ann Pamela Cunningham began a crusade to save George Washington's home, Mount Vernon. Five years later, following the first preservation campaign of national scope, her Mount Vernon Ladies Association of the Union won a charter that empowered it "to purchase, hold and improve" the property. Local patriots preserved Andrew Jackson's home, The Hermitage, outside Nashville, Tennessee, in 1889. The Governor's Palace in Santa Fe, New Mexico, was saved as a historic site in 1900. Paul Revere's house in Boston was restored in 1905.

In houses like Mount Vernon that had belonged to the nation's leaders, or in buildings like Independence Hall associated with historic events, it is easy to see the motivation behind the early preservation movement: patriotism. Such historic places were often called "shrines." And they were revered in an almost religious way.

By the late 19th and early 20th century, however, preservationists had begun to add another criterion: architectural design. Credit usually goes to William Sumner Appleton, who in 1910 founded the Society for the Preservation of New England Antiquities, the first regional historical society. (The Association for the Preservation of Virginia Antiquities, the first statewide preservation group, had been founded in 1888 with a more traditionally patriotic focus.) Appleton had two main concerns: a scholarly interpretation of history and architecture and opening houses as museums to teach the public about architecture, history and life in the past. Whether based in patriotism or design, house museums for decades remained the backbone of the American preservation movement. Thomas Jefferson's Monticello, preserved in 1923, combines both these concerns admirably. But then, Jefferson himself was America's best known Renaissance Man.

It wasn't long before preservation expanded even more. And each step included the historic house at its core.

* In 1927 Williamsburg, Virginia, backed by John D. Rockefeller, Jr., set out to save an entire city through massive and scholarly reconstruction and restoration.

* In 1931 Charleston, South Carolina, enacted the nation's first ordinance that used zoning as a tool to protect not only historic buildings but entire sections of the city. The local "Old and Historic Charleston District," which principally covered residential neighborhoods, was followed in 1936 by New Orleans' "Vieux Carre Historic District." In 1939, San Antonio enacted historic district zoning to protect "La Villita," an old neighborhood dating from Spanish colonial days.

* In 1932, The Natchez Garden Club in Mississippi conducted the first tour of historic homes, creating a showcase for historic homes that preservation societies around the country have imitated.

* Using Williamsburg as a model, Henry Ford began the Henry Ford Museum and Greenfield Village in Michigan in 1936. Other restored communities followed in the 1940s and 1950s: Old Sturbridge Village in Massachusetts, Old Salem in North Carolina, St. Augustine in Florida.

* In 1958 Charleston created the first revolving fund to buy endangered buildings and resell them for restoration. In the intervening years, uncounted hundreds of homes have been saved in this way around the country.

The years, however, have also been hard on historic homes. While patriotism, design, uniqueness and sheer age have encouraged preservation, they have not always guaranteed it, because, as the people who had built old homes died, their children and grandchildren often did not want yesterday's fashion. They had already moved to the newer suburbs being built at the end of the streetcar line or the freeway. As a result, old neighborhoods and old houses began to run down. By the 1960s, deterioration was severe in most cities. Then, from the depths of decay, people began to see the value of old houses again. Prompted by low prices and high design, the convenience to work downtown and the camaraderie of do-it-yourselfers all working on their old houses at the same time, thousands of Americans moved back into historic homes. Soon, warehouses were being turned into shopping centers, firehouses were being turned into restaurants and mills were being turned into offices. But the historic house had led the way.

That's because one central fact remains true about preservation. Namely, that no matter how many buildings are saved, and no matter how many new techniques are created for saving them, preservationists never give up on the old ways. The historic house is still a central fact of preservation, whether it stands alone or is part of a neighborhood. The earliest reasons for preservation, to inspire a sense of history and patriotism, are still valid, as are the goals of the next step, to preserve quality architectural design. Newer concerns emphasize community development or environmental conservation. But all provide touchstones with the past, a means of physically understanding and relating to history.

THE IMPORTANCE OF PRESERVATION

For more than 100 years, battles have been waged to save buildings associated with great men. Preservationists have also fought the war for stylish design. Sometimes their visions were a bit narrow. A guidebook for the Historic Charleston Foundation's homes tour in the mid-1950s, for example, derided "ghastly 'late' Victorianisms" and praised "the slow recovery of good taste after them." But without a vision, thousands of houses of all styles would have been lost. The pressures of metropolitan growth and rising real estate values have been enormous since the 1950s. Historic houses needed preservationists to channel that pressure into a movement that would restore rather than destroy them.

Today, preservation affects not only the homes of the famous but the homes of common folk. Preservation is a reminder that, like our natural resources, our historic resources are precious. Preservation reminds us that we must be good stewards of history. And preservation has taught us how to learn from our historic homes and other old buildings. Preservation can take at least partial credit for injecting the humane qualities inherent in old buildings into new construction.

Historic buildings give us our place in the landscape, because no two cities, towns, neighborhoods or family homes developed in exactly the same way. Sometimes the difference is obvious: New Mexico is not New York. But even when the natural landscape has more in common – say, between Maine and Oregon – the cultural landscape is different. Historic buildings also give us our place in history. They mirror the values of our ancestors. And of ourselves. They ask how we feel about our history. And about our present.

Besides, saving historic homes makes plain good sense, just like conserving and recycling natural resources. Rehabilitation is labor intensive, so you can save money on building materials. Old houses are often less expensive than new ones, plus you save the cost of buying undeveloped land. You can do much of the work yourself, phasing your project, even living in the house while you do the work.

Besides, once an old building's gone, it's gone forever.

That's why people who were "too poor to paint, too proud to whitewash" hung onto their property. They knew valuable history and valuable resources were there, under the dust, mildew and peeling paint, behind the weedy wisteria and sagging shutters. And they knew that someday they could bring their house back to life.

The fact is, preservation is as much about the future as it is about the past. Saving historic houses can preserve – or revive – more than architectural styles. It can preserve a way of life that all too often gets lost in the hustle and bustle that usually comes with modern design. Preservation is not just about saving a few buildings. It is ultimately about finding a useful role for old buildings today and allowing those old buildings to contribute to contemporary life.

So far, it seems to be working. Paul Goldberger, who succeeded Ada Louise Huxtable as *The Times'* architecture critic, has written:

"The preservation movement ... has helped reduce our culture's obsession with newness for its own sake."

The result? We can now get on with the business of building an America that is as diverse architecturally as it is culturally. And it all begins with historic houses.

Native American pueblo, Mexican Mission, German half timber, Georgian, Greek Revival, Italianate, Queen Anne, Eastlake or grand chateau. Houses tell the story of American architecture – and the American people – better than any other kind of building.

HAMILTON HOUSE, South Berwick, ME

Hamilton House (this page), a magnificent example of a Georgian country house, was built in 1718 for Colonel Jonathan Hamilton. In the 1840s, the house was bought by Emily Tyson, and was later bequeathed to the Society for the Preservation of New England Antiquities by her daughter. It is a National Historic Landmark, and tours of the both the house and the gardens are on offer.

Sayward-Wheeler House (facing page), now part of York Historic District, was bought by Jonathan Sayward, a local merchant and civic leader, in the 1760s. Sayward enlarged the original 1718 Georgian house and furnished its rooms with valuable pieces of furniture, many of which were imported from Europe. The beautifully-preserved house, now owned by the Society for the Preservation of New England Antiquities, is open to the public.

Governor John Langdon's fine 1783 mansion (facing page), now a National Historic Landmark open to the public, was admired by George Washington when he visited Portsmouth in 1789. He wrote in his diary that of all Portsmouth's houses "Colonel Langdon's may be esteemed the first." Descendants of the original owner commissioned Stanford White to add a wing around the turn of the century.

The clapperboard mansion (above), residence of New Hampshire's first royal governor, Benning Wentworth, in the 1750s, dates from 1695 and is a National Historic Landmark, open to the public.

HILDENE, Manchester Village, VT

Hildene (this page), the graceful Georgian Revival mansion that was the summer residence of Robert Todd Lincoln, was completed in 1904, and remained in the Lincoln family until 1975. The mansion – listed in the National Register of Historic Places – is now administered by the Friends of Hildene, and since 1979 has been open to the public as a house museum. Rooms on the first floor of the twenty-four-room mansion have been lovingly restored and are decorated as they would have been in Lincoln's era.

Justin Smith Morrill Homestead (facing page), a National Historic Landmark, was built in 1851 for U.S. representative and senator Justin Smith Morrill. It is an outstanding example of Gothic Revival architecture, boasting the steep, gabled roof and the elaborate, carved trim along the eaves that are characteristic of the style. The house, which is filled with family possessions, is open to the public.

In 1770 Colonel Josiah Quincy, a prominent leader in the War of Independence, built his house on a plot of land given to his great-grandfather by the colonial government in Boston. Visitors to the house, which is listed in the National Register of Historic Places, can see many features of the original house, including the moldings in the parlor (right) and the Liverpool tiles surrounding the fireplace in the dining room (below).

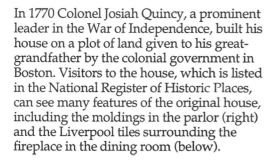

The clean lines and elegant proportions of eighteenth-century Sargent House are characteristic of the Georgian style of architecture. The house is sumptuously decorated and many rooms, including the dining room (above) and the parlor (left), are furnished with antiques.

Codman House, built in 1740, was enlarged by its new owner, John Codman, when he inherited it in the 1790s. The extension, in which many believe architect Charles Bulfinch had a hand, transformed the house into a three-story mansion. Its interior is filled with eighteenth- and nineteenth-century treasures, making it popular with visitors. In the mid-nineteenth century the back parlor was converted into an Elizabethan Revival dining room (below). Right: the library.

ROPES MANSION, Salem, MA

Though the exterior of Ropes Mansion has changed little since the house was built in 1727, the interior reflects the styles current in the nineteenth century, when it was renovated. The parlor (left) and the dining room (above) have recently been refurbished with reproductions of nineteenth-century wall coverings and carpets. Both the house, and the beautiful formal gardens that surround it, are now administered by the Essex Institute and are open to visitors.

MARK TWAIN HOUSE, Hartford, CT

Samuel Clemens, perhaps better known by his pen-name Mark Twain, spent more than $100,000 on the construction of his Hartford home. Designed by architects Edward T. Potter and Alfred H. Thorp, the 1874 house includes patterns in black and vermilion on its exterior walls, a steep roof, and numerous turrets and balconies, features which were considered extravagant even by Victorian standards. The house, which is a National Historic Landmark, is open to the public.

The 1864 Lockwood-Mathews Mansion, designed by architect Detlef Lienau for Le Grand Lockwood, a prominent financier and treasurer of the New York Stock Exchange, is now a National Historic Landmark, open to the public. The mansion is a fine example of high-Victorian architecture, with lavish decoration in its interior. The library (facing page) boasts a fine inlaid wooden floor and reflects the Victorian love of embellishment. Left: the richly-carved grand staircase.

Anti-slavery campaigner Harriet Beecher Stowe, famous for her work *Uncle Tom's Cabin*, lived with her husband and family in a pleasant house in the Nook Farm area of Hartford, a district very popular with writers and artists during the nineteenth century. The 1871 house, furnished with many of the author's possessions, is listed in the National Register of Historic Places and is open to the public

JOSEPH WEBB HOUSE, Wethersfield, CT

In 1781 George Washington met with Rochambeau – the commander of French forces in America – in the Joseph Webb House. The bedroom where Washington slept (left) and the room in which the two men met (above) have been accurately restored. The 1752 mansion, boasting many colonial elements, is now a National Historic Landmark, open to the public. Facing page: Henry C. Bowen Cottage was built in 1846 for Henry C. Bowen. The house – a masterly piece of Gothic Revival architecture designed by English architect Joseph Wells – is owned by the Society for the Preservation of New England Antiquities. It is listed in the National Register of Historic Places and is open to the public.

The small, two-and-a-half-story frame house where the renowned eighteenth-century portrait painter Gilbert Stuart was born, has been beautifully preserved. The 1751 house, now a National Historic Landmark, is furnished with pieces of period furniture, giving visitors a valuable insight into colonial life.

Governor Sprague Mansion, a twenty-eight-room building completed in 1790, was home to several generations of the wealthy and politically-powerful Sprague family. The original eighteenth-century house was enlarged in 1864, when William Sprague was serving in the U.S. Senate. The house is listed in the National Register of Historic Places, and is open to the public by appointment.

CHATEAU-SUR-MER, Newport, RI

When Chateau-sur-Mer was built in 1852 for William Shepard Wetmore, it was the first of the large houses on Bellevue Avenue, and its grandeur quickly became a benchmark for other Newport mansions. The original building, designed by architect Seth Bradford, was enlarged in 1872 by Richard Morris Hunt, with only the ballroom (above) remaining unaltered. The mansion is listed in the National Register of Historic Places, and is open to the public.

BLITHEWOLD, Bristol, RI

The estate of Blithewold in Bristol, Rhode Island, was bought by Augustus Van Wickle in 1894. It was not until 1907, however, that his family built the pleasant, forty-five-room house that exists today. The house was included in the National Register of Historic Places in 1980. Left: the dining room, furnished in the nineteenth-century style. Top left: the elegant master bedroom.

The Elms, a gracious, French-style mansion designed by famous architect Horace Trumbauer, was built in 1901 for Pennsylvania coal magnate Edward J. Berwind. Berwind, who was considered *nouveau riche* by the established Newport families, decorated his home with an opulence to rival theirs. The mansion, listed in the National Register of Historic Places, is now a house museum, attracting many visitors.

The Hunter House, built in 1748 for Jonathan Nichols, Deputy Governor of Rhode Island, is a National Historic Landmark, open to the public. Among the most impressive of Rhode Island's eighteenth-century mansions, it is beautifully preserved and maintained, and boasts a superb collection of period furnishings.

THE BREAKERS, Newport, RI

Many of the most famous Newport homes were designed by Richard Morris Hunt. His design for The Breakers (facing page), the palatial summer residence of Cornelius Vanderbilt II, is based on a northern Italian *palazzo*. The 1895 mansion, like 1892 Marble House (above and right) – another of Hunt's designs – is listed in the National Register of Historic Places, and is now a house museum.

Boscobel, included in the National Register of Historic Places in 1977, was built in 1804, and is a magnificent example of New York Federal architecture. The house was threatened by developers in the 1950s and was moved, section by section, to a site fifteen miles to the north and reconstructed there. Since 1961, the lovingly-restored mansion, has been open to the public.

WESTBURY HOUSE, Old Westbury, NY

Westbury House (these pages), built in 1903, is reminiscent of an English country estate. The home of Mr. and Mrs. John S. Phipps for over fifty years, it was opened to the public in 1959. Both the house and garden have been beautifully maintained, giving visitors a glimpse of the gracious lifestyle for which Long Island is renowned. Facing page: the elegant oak-paneled dining room. Left: the charming White Drawing Room.

Van Cortlandt Manor (these pages), which remained in the Van Cortlandt family – one of New York's most influential – until 1945, is now a National Historic Landmark. One of five properties maintained by Historic Hudson Valley, the 1749 house is beautifully restored and furnished. Much of the furniture once belonged to the family, and gives visitors to the property an accurate picture of changing styles and tastes.

THE ABBEY, Cape May, NJ

The parlor (left) and dining room (above) of the Abbey, summer residence of the nineteenth-century coal baron, John McCreary, are decorated in the high-Victorian style and are filled with antiques. The 1869 house, part of Cape May Historic District – a National Historic Landmark – is now a bed and breakfast inn. Tours of the property are available.

Queen Victoria Inn (facing page), an 1881 villa now run as a bed and breakfast inn, is one of the many fine Victorian buildings in the seaside resort of Cape May. The town, which became fashionable in the nineteenth century, was restored in the 1960s and has now been designated a National Historic Landmark.

The Emlen Physick Estate, designed by architect Frank Furness in 1879, is one of Cape May's treasures. It was due for demolition when it was announced that the town was listed in the National Register of Historic Places. The house, restored and now administered by the Mid-Atlantic Center for the Arts, is open to the public.

HARTWOOD ACRES, Pittsburg, PA

Hartwood Acres, a beautiful re-creation of a Tudor mansion, was designed in the 1930s by architect Alfred Hopkins, for John and Mary Flinn Lawrence. Its Great Hall (facing page) boasts a carved oak fireplace dating from 1620, and antique Georgian furniture.

FORT HUNTER MANSION, Harrisburg, PA

Fort Hunter Mansion, built in 1814 by Archibald MacAllister, is a fine example of the Federal style of architecture that became popular after the Revolution. The mansion, built on a strategically important site near the Susquehanna River, is open to the public, and offers a fine collection of period furniture and costumes.

The Boal Mansion, home to nine successive generations of the Boal family, dates from 1789 and is listed in the National Register of Historic Places. Above: the ballroom, added in 1898 when the family farm became the family estate. Right: the ornately-decorated hallway.

ROLAND CURTIN MANSION, Bellefonte, PA

Roland Curtin Mansion (above) was built in 1830 for Roland Curtin, the owner and founder of the Eagle Ironworks. The fifteen-room Federal-style mansion, now listed in the National Register of Historic Places, has been carefully restored, and is open to the public. The elegant home of John Harris (facing page), founder of Harrisburg, Pennsylvania, was later owned by Simon Cameron, an influential nineteenth-century politician. The original house, built by Harris between 1764 and 1766, was enlarged in the 1860s. The house is a National Historic Landmark and is open to the public.

JOHN HARRIS-SIMON CAMERON HOUSE, Harrisburg, PA

The Strawberry Mansion (this page), built in 1789 for Judge William Lewis, was expanded in the 1920s, when two wings were added. The interior of the house is decorated in the Empire, Regency and Federal styles.

Sweetbriar (facing page), built in 1797, is a near-perfect example of the Federal style of architecture. Its design is refined, delicate and clean cut.

GEORGE READ II HOUSE, New Castle, DE

Work on the home of George Read II, a prominent citizen of New Castle, started in 1765, following plans made by Peter Crouding, a Philadelphia carpenter. The elegant house, which Read intended to be the grandest home in the state, was not completed until 1804. The mansion, part of New Castle Historic District – a National Historic Landmark – was bequeathed to the Historical Society of Delaware in 1975 and, after ten years of careful research and painstaking restoration, it was opened to the public. Left: the basement tap room. Below: the rear parlor.

ELEUTHERIAN MILLS, Hagley, DE

Eleutherian Mills, a Georgian-style country mansion located near the Brandywine River, was the home of the du Pont family for five generations. The 1802 house, its charming grounds, and the yards of the family's successful black powder business are now part of the Hagley Museum, a National Historic Landmark. Visitors to the museum are given a unique insight into industrial and domestic life during the nineteenth century.

Nineteenth-century Homewood, now a registered National Historic Landmark, was a wedding gift from Charles Carroll to his son Charles Carroll, Junior and his wife, Harriet. In the records relating to the house, no mention is made of a professional architect, and many believe that Charles Carroll, Junior designed the mansion himself. The magnificent house, which cost nearly $40,000 to build, has been restored to its former glory by Johns Hopkins University and is open to the public. Researchers used the family's house inventories and estate sale catalogues to ensure that all rooms in the house were furnished authentically.

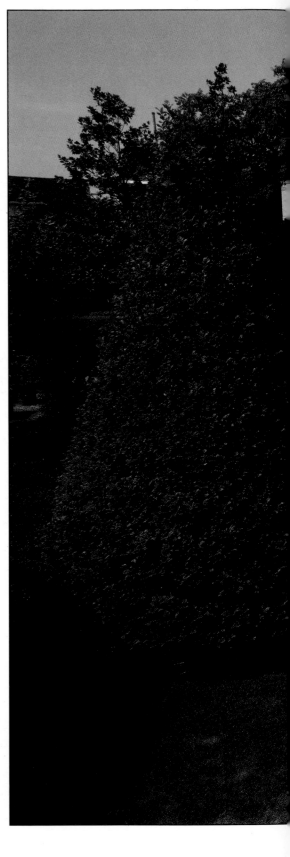

William Paca House, in Annapolis, was built in 1765 for a former governor of Maryland, William Paca. The house, which had been converted into a hotel in the early twentieth century, was only saved from demolition in 1965 by the decisive action of Historic Annapolis. Visitors to the house, a National Historic Landmark, are charmed both by the elegant mansion, and by the recreation of Governor Paca's original formal garden.

HAMPTON, Towson, MD

Hampton – listed in the National Register of Historic Places, and open to the public – was built between 1783 and 1790 and is among the largest Georgian-style mansions in Maryland. The house was home to the Ridgely family until 1948, and its interior reflects different eras of the family's occupancy. The dining room (facing page) is decorated as it would have been c.1810-1830, with the woodwork painted blue and details picked out in ochre. The music room (left) is decorated in the Victorian fashion.

On his return from France in 1789, Thomas Jefferson began work on redesigning Monticello (these pages), his 1770 Virginia home. He departed from the style of architecture current in early eighteenth-century America, employing aspects of design he had seen in Europe, including a classical dome and a single classical portico. The house, a National Historic Landmark, is architecturally one of America's most significant buildings and is perhaps Virginia's most popular tourist attraction.

Nineteenth-century Oatlands, one of the properties listed in the National Register of Historic Places, belongs to the National Trust for Historic Preservation, and is open to visitors from early spring until late fall. The house was designed and built by George Carter, and remained in the Carter family from 1810, when it was completed, until 1897. Above: the dining room. Right: the main hall.

Mount Vernon, built in 1743 by Augustine Washington in idyllic surroundings on the banks of the Potomac River, was much loved by his son, George Washington. After George Washington's death the estate became increasingly unproductive and, after attempts to persuade the Federal government to buy and restore it had failed, it was sold to the Mount Vernon Ladies Association. The association has maintained and administered the property, a National Historic Landmark, since 1858.

Tryon Palace, a beautiful Georgian red-brick mansion, was designed by English architect John Hawks and was constructed between 1767 and 1770. A fire in 1798 destroyed much of the house, with only the stable wing surviving intact. It was reconstructed in the 1950s on the original foundations, and was decorated with period furnishings. It is now open to the public.

Orton Plantation (facing page), near Wilmington, is famous for its beautiful gardens. In the spring wisteria, azaleas and other flowering plants turn the grounds into a mass of color. The original house, which was built in 1725 for Roger Moore, was enlarged in 1910 when two wings were added. Though listed on the National Register of Historic Places, the house is not accessible to the public.

Biltmore (this page), built between 1890 and 1895, was designed by Richard Morris Hunt for George Washington Vanderbilt. The 250-room mansion, based on a sixteenth-century French chateau, is the largest private residence in the United States. It is a National Historic Landmark and is open to the public.

HEYWARD-WASHINGTON HOUSE, Charleston, SC

Thomas Heyward, a signer of the Declaration of Independence, inherited the elegant 1770 townhouse (this page), in Church Street, Charleston, from his father. The house, a National Historic Landmark, is now owned by Charleston Museum and is open to the public. It has been beautifully restored, and boasts a wealth of eighteenth-century furnishings.

Nathaniel Russell House (facing page), a National Historic Landmark accessible to the public, was built for one of Charleston's leading merchants, Nathaniel Russell. The 1809 house is a fine example of the Federal style, offering features such as the fan-shaped window above the door

JOSEPH MANIGAULT HOUSE, Charleston, SC

Joseph Manigault House, a Federal-style masterpiece, was built in 1790 for Joseph Manigault, a wealthy planter. The three-story mansion, designed by his brother Gabriel Manigault, was a radical departure in style from single- or two-story buildings more traditional in Charleston. Its interior is beautifully furnished with pieces made by local craftsmen. The house is a National Historic Landmark, open to the public.

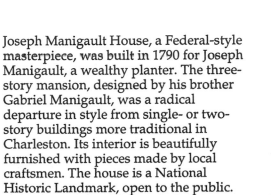

MIDDLETON PLACE, Nr. Charleston, SC

Middleton Place (this page), dating from 1741, was set ablaze by Sherman's troops during the Civil War, and only a fraction of the original house was rebuilt. Though much of the family's furniture was lost either to the fire or to Union soldiers, a few pieces have survived and remain in the house. The house is a National Historic Landmark and is open to the public.

Drayton Hall (facing page), a National Historic Landmark, was built between 1738 and 1742. The house, a fine example of early Georgian architecture, remained in the Drayton family until 1974, when it was purchased by the National Trust for Historic Preservation and opened to the public.

For many, Boone Hall Plantation (this page) is the epitome of a Southern plantation. Visitors approach the house – a 1930s Georgian-style mansion similar to the original mansion – along an avenue of oak trees.

Wedge Plantation (facing page), near Charleston, was built in 1826. The plantation's fine gardens boast magnolia trees planted by the builder over one hundred years ago.

The 1885 Lapham-Patterson House (facing page), elaborate, and asymmetrical in its design, is considered an architectural jewel and was designated a National Historical Landmark in 1975.

Unlike other Thomasville homes, the mansion is open to the public. The 1841 Susina Plantation (above), designed by architect John Wind, has been meticulously restored. The design of the house – which is listed in the National Register of Historic Places – includes Ionic columns and a pediment, features that are characteristic of the Greek-Revival style.

JULIETTE GORDON LOW HOUSE, Savannah, GA

Juliette Gordon Low House, a lovely Regency-style mansion designed by William Jay, was built in 1818 for James M. Wayne. A National Historic Landmark, it has been restored to its 1870s appearance and is open to the public as a memorial to Juliette Gordon Low, the founder of the Girl Scouts of America.

Pebble Hill, near the popular nineteenth-century winter resort of Thomasville, was designed in 1936 by Abram Garfield, son of President James A. Garfield. Pebble Hill Plantation – the third plantation house on the site – was included in the National Register of Historic Places in 1990 and is open every day for guided tours.

FORT CONDE-CHARLOTTE HOUSE, Mobile, AL

Fort Conde-Charlotte House (this page), dating from 1820, is listed in the National Register of Historic Places. Rooms in the house, which has been restored by the National Society of Colonial Dames of America in the State of Alabama and is open to the public as a museum, have been authentically decorated to represent different eras in the town's history.

Dean Page Hall (facing page) — one of the many reminders of Eufaula's prosperous past — is among a number of the buildings in the town listed in the National Register of Historic Places. The large, elegant 1850 mansion is not open to the public. Perhaps its most unusual feature is its rooftop lookout point.

STURDIVANT HALL, Selma, AL

Work on Sturdivant Hall began in 1853 and took almost three years to complete. The mansion, a Neo-Classical gem built by Thomas Helm Lee, is one of the finest surviving antebellum houses in Selma, and is listed on the National Register of Historic Places. The house is open to the public, and visitors can admire the artistry of the craftsmen who were brought in to work on the interior of the house. The plaster ceilings and the ornate vine-and-grape-leaf moldings are of particular note.

Bluff Hall, listed in the National Register of Historic Places and open to the public, is built on cliffs high above the Tombigbee River. The magnificent Greek-Revival columns, which so dominate the exterior of the mansion, were added to the original Federal-style brick building in 1840, eight years after it had been completed. The interior of the mansion is furnished in the Empire and the mid-Victorian styles.

Gaineswood, the elegant antebellum house built for General Nathan Bryan Whitfield, was completed in 1860, having taken a period of almost eighteen years to construct. Its design reflects the changing fashions in architecture which took place in the nineteenth century, from Greek Revival to Renaissance Revival to Italianate. The mansion, a National Historic Landmark, was acquired by the State of Alabama in 1966. It has been meticulously restored and is open to the public.

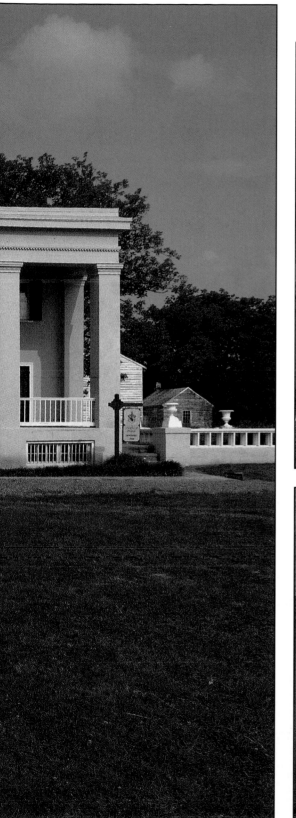

Melrose (above), built in 1845 for John T. McMurran, is one of the best-preserved of the Natchez Mississippi plantations. Expense was no object for McMurran, and the money he lavished on his home – now a National Historic Landmark open to the public – is apparent in the furnishings in its interior. The drawing room (right) boasts intricately-carved rosewood furniture, brocatelle draperies, gilt mirrors, and an ornate chandelier.

Work on Longwood (facing page), an eight-sided brick-faced "Oriental Villa" designed by Samuel Sloan for Haller Nutt, was begun in 1860. Its ornate exterior was finished by 1861 and work had begun on the interior of the ground floor when the Civil War finally brought construction to a halt. The house, a National Historic Landmark, was presented to the Pilgrimage Garden Club in 1970, and is open to the public.

CEDAR GROVE, Vicksburg, MS

Cedar Grove, in Vicksburg, is an attractive two-story Greek-Revival mansion dating from the 1840s. The mansion, which is set amid beautiful formal gardens, was included in the National Register of Historic Places in 1982. Though it has been converted into a hotel, guided tours are still available.

Architectural ideas picked up by Martha and Daniel Turnbull while they were on honeymoon in Europe were incorporated into the design of their home, Rosedown Plantation. Though the house was not large, the Turnbulls were determined that its style and workmanship should be unsurpassed in the state. The skill of the local carpenter-builder who worked on the 1835 house is still apparent to visitors.

San Francisco Plantation, near Reserve, in Louisiana, is unique in its design, combining features of different architectural styles. The house was built in 1850 by Edmond Bozonier Marmillion, and its interior is furnished as it would have been in this era. The mansion, a National Historic Landmark, has now been made into a museum.

Nottoway, a magnificent 1859 plantation home near Baton Rouge, Louisiana, is now a restaurant and inn. The mansion, an imposing blend of Greek Revival and Italianate styles, was designed by Henry Howard, one of the nineteenth century's most successful architects, and is in the National Register of Historic Places.

Ashton Villa, in Galveston, Texas, was saved from demolition in the 1960s by the Galveston Historical Foundation and is now open as a museum. The Italianate-style house, listed in the National Register of Historic Places, was built in 1859 by James Moreau Brown, a wealthy and prominent citizen of Galveston. It was a family home, and many of the Browns' possessions still remain in the house today, recreating the atmosphere of the house in the nineteenth century.

GOVERNOR'S MANSION, Austin, TX

The Governor's Mansion – listed in the National Register of Historic Places and open to the public – is an impressive Greek-Revival building, boasting magnificent Ionic columns made of cypress and pine. The house, built by Abner Cook, a master builder, was completed in 1856, having taken nearly two years to construct.

Shriver House is another of the elegant, Greek-Revival mansions found in Austin. Both the exterior of the house and its opulent interior are in keeping with the Southern tradition.

ESTEVAN HALL, Helena, AR

Estevan Hall – listed in the National Register of Historic Places and open to the public by appointment – is magnificently situated, offering a fine view of the Mississippi River from its long porch. The house, built in 1826 for Fleetwood Hanks, a local plantation owner, has remained in the family ever since. The interior of the house (above left and left) is lavishly decorated.

Rosalie, built in 1883 for Mr. and Mrs. J. W. Hill, is one of the most beautiful mansions in the popular nineteenth-century spa resort of Eureka Springs. The mansion, with a large encircling verandah, bay windows and turrets, is an exuberant mixture of the Queen Anne and Carpenter Gothic styles. The furnishings, original to the house, are typical of the period. The mansion, part of the Eureka Springs Historic District – listed in the National Register of Historic Places – is open to the public.

BONNEVILLE, Fort Smith, AR

Bonneville (this page), a charming 1864 mansion, was bought in 1887 by the widow of General Benjamin Bonneville. The house, listed in the National Register of Historic Places, is one of a number of historically significant buildings in Fort Smith's Belle Grove Historic District.

Pillow-Thompson House (facing page) – listed in the National Register of Historic Places – was built in the late 1890s. It is a Queen Anne masterpiece, with elaborate turrets and pediments.

THE HERMITAGE, Nashville, TN

The Hermitage (this page), a beautiful 1819 Federal-style building, was the home of Andrew Jackson, the seventh president of the United States. In 1889, thirty-three years after the house had been purchased by the state, the Ladies Hermitage Site was formed with the aim of preserving the site. It is now a National Historic Landmark, open to the public.

James Knox Polk House (facing page), a National Historic Landmark, was built in 1816 by Samuel Polk, father of President James K. Polk. The house is now a museum dedicated to the memory of the president, and is filled with pieces of furniture that were used by the Polks during their time in the White House.

Belle Meade, listed in the National Register of Historic Places, is a fine 1853 Greek-Revival mansion. Throughout most of the nineteenth century the estate was renowned as a thoroughbred horse-breeding farm. Now a property of the Association for the Preservation of Tennessee Antiquities, Belle Meade is open to the public as a museum.

OAKLANDS, Murfreesboro, TN

Oaklands (this page), begun in 1818, was built over a period of forty years, and its design combines aspects of the Federal and Italianate styles. The house – listed in the National Register of Historic Places – is now a museum, and its interior is furnished as it would have been in 1862, giving an indication of the comfortable lifestyle enjoyed by its inhabitants.

Rattle and Snap (facing page) is one of the best examples of Greek Revival architecture in America. The 1845 mansion, built for George W. Polk, boasts a graceful portico supported by ten Corinthian columns. The house, a National Historic Landmark, is privately owned and is not accessible to the public.

White Hall, designed by architects Lewinski and McMurtry, was constructed in 1799 for Cassius Marcellus Clay – later a minister to Russia. The mansion, a brick-built house in the Italianate style, with three stories on five levels, is listed in the National Register of Historic Places and is open to the public.

FARMINGTON, Louisville, KY

Farmington (this page), built in 1810 for John and Lucy Fry Speed, is listed in the National Register of Historic Places and is open to the public. The mansion, symmetrical and harmonious in its design, is a beautiful example of the Jeffersonian Classical style, which adapted the architectural ideas of Thomas Jefferson.

Ward Hall (facing page), among the finest Greek-Revival mansions in America, was completed in 1853. The house replaced an earlier 1817 structure, and used materials from it, including the door lintel. At one time it was proposed that the mansion be used as the Kentucky State Capitol. The house, listed in the National Register of Historic Places, is now open to the public.

Avery-Downer House, a Greek-Revival mansion constructed in 1842, now houses the Robbins Hunter Museum. Fourteen of the mansion's twenty-seven rooms are open to the public, displaying a magnificent collection of eighteenth- and nineteenth-century furniture and paintings. Facing page: the gentlemen's parlor.

Adena, a Georgian-style mansion listed in the National Register of Historic Places, was designed by architect Benjamin H. Latrobe. The elegant, two-story house, home of Thomas Worthington, a prominent figure in early Ohio politics, was completed in 1807. The mansion is now open to the public, and its interior, including the dining room (above right) and the kitchen (right), has been restored to its early nineteenth-century appearance.

ABBIE & GENEVIEVE SCHOENBERGER HOUSE, Ludington, MI

Abbie and Genevieve Schoenberger House, in Ludington, was built in 1903 for Warren Cartier, a local lumberman, and is still maintained as a private residence. The interior of the house is lavishly decorated with woods such as oak and black cherry. Left: the hallway. Facing page: the dining room.

The design of 1860 Honolulu House (these pages), originally the home of Judge Abner Pratt, former U.S. consul to Hawaii, reflects his love of the Hawaiian Islands. Features such as the raised veranda and the observation platform are typical of Polynesian design. The house, now listed in the National Register of Historic Places, has been restored by the Marshall Historical Society to its 1880 appearance, and is open to the public.

Morris-Butler House, in Indianapolis, a Second Empire Italianate villa built in 1864, was designed by Diedrich A. Bohlen and is listed in the National Register of Historic Places. The mansion, now a house museum, boasts a superb collection of Victoriana. A Wooten desk, typical of the "industrial style" furniture made in the town, stands in Noble Butler's office (right). Above: the library, which adjoins the dining room.

John J. Glessner House, on Chicago's prestigious Prairie Avenue, was one of the last – and perhaps most influential – works of Boston architect Henry Hobson Richardson. The house, which was completed in 1887, has a fortress-like exterior that opens onto an inner courtyard (facing page). Rooms at the front of the house, like the schoolroom (left), have small windows, while those at the rear, like the library (above), have larger windows. The house, a National Historic Landmark, is open to the public.

Terrace Hill, designed by architect William W. Boyington, was commissioned by nineteenth-century millionaire Benjamin F. Allen in 1867. When, only seventeen years later, Allen lost his fortune, he was forced to sell the elaborate Second Empire mansion. Since 1976, the house, which is listed in the National Register of Historic Places and is accessible to the public, has been the Governor of Iowa's residence.

Cupples House, in St. Louis, one of the best examples of Richardson Romanesque architecture, was built in 1890 for Samuel Cupples. The mansion, listed in the National Register of Historic Places, is now owned by St. Louis University and open to the public. It boasts many treasures, including Galeazzo Campi's painting of the Nativity, which hangs on the wall of the library (right), and genuine French Empire furnishings in the dining room (above).

Oakland's Dunsmuir House, a magnificent thirty-seven-room mansion designed by Eugene Freeman, was built in 1899. The estate, which is set in the East Bay foothills, was purchased by I.W. Hellman in 1906, shortly after the death of Alexander Dunsmuir and his wife Josephine. It remained in the Hellman family until 1959, when it was bought by the City of Oakland and opened to the public. The house is listed in the National Register of Historic Places.

McCONAGHY HOUSE, Hayward, CA

McConaghy House, a fine, twelve-room, Victorian farmhouse, was built by Neil McConaghy in 1886, and remained in his family until 1972. The house, which has been fully restored, is now run by the Hayward Area Historical Society and is open to the public. Right: the dining room, festooned with Easter decorations. Top right: the front parlor.

Construction of the Petaluma Adobe, a two-story building made of unburnt, sun-dried brick, began in 1834, under the direction of General Mariano Vallejo. The adobe, a National Historic Landmark, was once the headquarters of a 64,000-acre ranch. Though only one wing of the original adobe remains, it is still vast. Its interior, including rooms such as the dining room (left) and the weaving room (facing page) – which is filled with historical and crafts exhibits – gives visitors an insight into life in California during the Mexican period.

Haas-Lilienthal House (facing page), built in 1886, is a fine example of the Eastlake-Queen Anne style. The house, one of San Francisco's Victorian treasures, is listed in the National Register of Historic Places and is accessible to the public.

G.W. Patterson House (above), now part of Ardenwood Historic Farm, was designed by Samuel Newsom, an early proponent of the Queen Anne style. The house was included in the National Register of Historic Places in 1985.

The Phineas Banning Residence, a twenty-three-room mansion built in the Greek Revival style, was completed in 1864. The house, listed in the National Register of Historic Places, is now a museum. Its interior has been carefully restored, and furnishings include pieces owned by the Bannings. Left: the family living room. Above left: the parlor, containing laminated rosewood furniture.

Sam Brannan Cottage (above and right), part of the Sharpsteen Museum, is listed in the National Register of Historic Places and is open to the public. The 1860 cottage was one of several cottages built by Brannan in Calistoga, in his promotion of the spa town as a vacation resort. Many of the furnishings in the house, like those in the parlor (right), are original. Facing page: Lachryma Montis, the 1852 home of General Mariano Guadalupe Vallejo, is now open to the public as a museum.

MOREY MANSION, Redlands, CA

The 1890 Morey Mansion (above), originally owned by David Morey, a retired shipbuilder, is now run as an inn. Though basically constructed in the Queen Anne style, it borrows some features of other architectural styles. These include an onion-shaped dome and Gothic windows. Heritage House (facing page), a Queen Anne masterpiece designed by John H. Walls, was built in 1892 for James Bettner. The beautifully-restored house is listed in the National Register of Historic Places and is open to the public. It is now administered by the Riverside Municipal Museum.

John Bidwell's beautiful 1860 Italianate villa, Bidwell Mansion, stands on the banks of Chico Creek, in the upper Sacramento Valley. The twenty-six-room house was designed by architect Henry W. Cleaveland and boasted all the conveniences on offer in the 1860s, including gas lighting and plumbing. The mansion, listed in the National Register of Historic Places, has been lovingly restored, and is open to the public. Above right: the master bedroom. Right: the library.

Villa Montezuma, designed by architects Comstock and Trotsche, was built in 1887 for the author and musician Jesse Shepard. The two-story house boasts features such as a dome tower and turrets that are characteristic of the Queen Anne style of architecture. Today the house is listed in the National Register of Historic Places and is maintained as an historic house museum.